Let's Write!

Scott Foresman
Practice Station
Flip Chart

Reading STREET

Grade **3**

ISBN-13: 978-0-328-51572-1
ISBN-10: 0-328-51572-8

ISBN-13: 978-328-51572-1
ISBN-10:   328-51572-8
9 10 V0B4 14

Let's Write!

Narrative Poem

15 min.

You will need
- paper
- pencils

● Think of a time when you had a lot of fun. Write a narrative poem that tells about this time. Include a sensory detail that tells how something felt, looked, smelled, tasted, or sounded.

▲ Think of a time when you had a lot of fun. Write a narrative poem telling about this time. Use sensory details to help with your descriptions.

■ Recall a fun or special experience, and write a narrative poem that tells about it. Use sensory details to help your readers imagine they are there. Try to include a few lines of rhyme.

Let's Write!

Comic Books

15 min.

You will need

- paper
- pencils
- markers

● Write a short, four-picture comic book that tells the story of two characters. Write a plot that has a beginning, middle, and end. Draw pictures to go with your story.

▲ Write a short, four-picture comic book that tells the story of two characters. Write a plot that has a beginning, middle, and end. Draw pictures to go with your story.

■ Write a four- or six-picture comic book that tells about an adventure two characters have. Include dialogue and a plot with a beginning, middle, and end. Draw pictures that help tell the story.

Let's Write!

Narrative Poem

15 min.

You will need
- paper
- pencils

● Think of a time when you did not know what to expect. Write a narrative poem that tells about it. Include details that tell how things felt, looked, smelled, tasted, or sounded.

▲ Think of a time when you did not know what would happen next. Write a narrative poem that tells about this time. Use sensory details to help with your descriptions.

■ Recall a fun experience, and write a narrative poem that tells about it. Use sensory details to help your readers imagine the experience. Try to appeal to three different senses.

Let's Write!

Description

15 min.

You will need
- paper
- pencils

● Think about a place you have visited. Write sentences that tell about the place. Use sensory words that describe details about it. Proofread your description. Focus on word choice.

▲ Think of a place you have visited and write sentences to describe it. Use sensory words that tell about it. Proofread your description and focus on word choice.

■ Write a description telling about a place you have visited. Provide details that include sensory words that tell about this place. Proofread your description and focus on your word choice.

Let's Write!

Fable

You will need
- paper
- pencils

15 min.

● Write a short fable that teaches a lesson. Give your fable a title and tell about the setting. Check to see that you have used correct spelling and punctuation.

▲ Write a short fable that teaches a lesson. Tell about the setting in your fable, and give your fable a title. Check to see that you have used correct spelling and punctuation.

■ Write a short fable that teaches a lesson. Give your fable a title, and include details that tell about the fable's setting. Check to see that both your spelling and punctuation are correct.

Limericks

You will need
- paper
- pencils

15 min.

● Write a funny limerick. Remember that a limerick is a humorous, five-line poem. The first, second, and fifth lines rhyme. The third line rhymes with the fourth line.

▲ Write a humorous limerick. Remember a limerick is a funny, five-line poem. The first, second, and fifth lines rhyme. The third line rhymes with the fourth line.

■ Write a funny limerick that rhymes the first, second, and fifth lines. Remember that a limerick also rhymes the third line with the fourth line. Proofread to check word organization.

Let's Write!

Thank-You Letter

15 min.

You will need
- paper
- pencils

● Think of someone who has helped you. Write a thank-you letter to this person. Tell this person why you are thankful. Check to see that you have used commas correctly.

▲ Think of someone who has helped you, and write this person a thank-you letter. Tell why you are thankful and check to see that you have used commas correctly.

■ Write a thank-you letter to someone who has helped you in some way. Include details that tell why you are thankful and check your letter to make sure you have used commas correctly.

Let's Write!

Take Notes

15 min.

You will need
- paper
- pencils

● Choose and read a book provided by your teacher. As you read, take notes about the main idea and important details. Paraphrase ideas in the text. Include key words and phrases in your notes.

▲ Choose and read a book provided by your teacher. Take notes about the main idea and some important details. Paraphrase the text in your own words. Include key phrases and words.

■ Choose a book provided by your teacher. As you read, take notes about the main idea and important details. Paraphrase the text, using your own words. Include key words and phrases as well.

Let's Write!

Description

15 min.

You will need
- paper
- pencils

● Think about your favorite food. Write three sentences that describe this food. Tell about how it tastes, smells, looks, feels, or even sounds. Use words that let your personality come through.

▲ Write a short paragraph that describes your favorite food. Use sensory words to tell how the food tastes, looks, feels, smells, or sounds. Use a writing voice that shows your personality.

■ Write a paragraph describing your favorite food. Use sensory words in your description. Use a writing voice that reflects your personality.

Let's Write!

Book Review

15 min.

You will need
- paper
- pencils

● Think about a book you have read. Write a book review that tells your opinion of the book. Include details that will be helpful to readers. Underline the book's title.

▲ Write a review of a book you have read. Tell who wrote the book, and underline the title. Give your opinion of the book and include details that will be helpful to readers.

■ Write the title and the author of a book you've read. Think about what happens in the book. Think of an interesting way to begin your review and then write a summary of the book. Tell readers why or why not they should read it.

Let's Write!

Realistic Story

15 min.

You will need
- paper
- pencils

● Write a realistic story that tells about a student who does something to help a friend. Check to be sure that all of your sentences are complete.

▲ Write a realistic story that tells about a student who does something to help a relative or friend. Include a variety of short sentences and compound sentences.

■ Write a realistic story that tells about a student who does something to help a friend or relative. Include a variety of short sentences and compound sentences.

Let's Write!

Invitation

15 min.

You will need
- paper
- pencils

● Imagine you are having a party. Think of a friend you would like to invite. Write an invitation to your party. Tell the reason for the party. Include the time the party will start and end. Use colons in your start time and end time.

▲ Imagine you are having a party. Write an invitation to a friend. Include the reason for your party, and tell when the party will start and end. Use colons in your start time and end time.

■ Write an invitation to an imaginary party you are hosting. Include information telling when the party will start and end. Use colons when writing times. Tell the reason you are celebrating.

Let's Write!

Poem

15 min.

You will need
- paper
- pencils

● Write a short poem about a favorite person or pet. Choose words that tell why this person or pet is so special.

▲ Write a four- or five-line poem about a favorite person or pet. Choose words that give details about this favorite person or pet.

■ Write a poem about a favorite person or pet. Choose words that give details about this person or pet and explain why they are so special.

Let's Write!

Free-Verse Poem

15 min.

You will need
- paper
- pencils

● Think about your first time at a new place. Write a free-verse poem that tells your feelings about this time. Choose words that will help your readers imagine the experience and understand how you felt.

▲ Write a free-verse poem that tells about your first time at a new place. Choose words to help your readers understand how you felt. Include details that will help them imagine they are there.

■ Write a free-verse poem telling about your experience in a new situation. Use figurative language to help readers understand how you felt. Include details to help readers imagine the experience.

Let's Write!

Fairy Tale

15 min.

You will need
- paper
- pencils

● Write a short fairy tale that tells about solving a problem. Use at least two vivid verbs that describe the tale's action. Circle these verbs.

▲ Write a short fairy tale that uses vivid verbs and tells about solving a problem. Include at least four vivid verbs. Circle the vivid verbs.

■ Write a fairy tale that tells about solving a difficult problem. Include at least five vivid verbs and five carefully chosen words. Circle the verbs and the carefully chosen words.

Let's Write!

Personal Narrative

15 min.

You will need
- paper
- pencils

● Think about an important event in your life. Write a personal narrative describing it. Include details about how the event made you feel. Use the pronoun *I* in your narrative.

▲ Write a personal narrative telling about an important event in your life. Describe the event and include details about your feelings. Use a consistent verb tense throughout your narrative.

■ Write a personal narrative describing an important event in your life. Include details about how the event made you feel. Use a consistent verb tense throughout your narrative.

Let's Write!

Persuasive Advertisement

15 min.

You will need
- paper
- pencil
- crayons or markers

● Write an advertisement for a place you like to visit. Tell what makes this place so great. Include a sentence that persuades others to visit. Illustrate your ad.

▲ Write an advertisement for a place you like to visit and explain what makes this place so great. Include three sentences that persuade others to visit. Illustrate your ad.

■ Think of a place you like to visit, and write an advertisement that tells what makes this place so great. Include a short paragraph that persuades others to visit. Illustrate your ad.

Let's Write!

Letter to the Editor

15 min.

You will need
- paper
- pencils

● Think of a problem in your school or community. Write a letter to the editor about this problem. Explain the problem and give details. Tell what you think should be done about this problem.

▲ Write a letter to the editor about a problem in your school or community. Explain the problem and give details. Tell what you think should be done about this problem.

■ Write a letter to the editor about a problem in your school or community. Explain the problem and provide details about it. Tell what you think should be done to solve this problem.

Let's Write!

Friendly Letter

15 min.

You will need
- paper
- pencils

● Imagine you are a character in *Tops & Bottoms*. Write a friendly letter to another character. Tell what you have been doing lately.

▲ Imagine you are a character in *Tops & Bottoms*. Write a friendly letter to another character. Tell what you have been doing. Include the date, a salutation, and a closing.

■ Imagine you are a character in *Tops & Bottoms*. Write a friendly letter to another character. Ask questions and describe what you have been doing. Include the date, a salutation, and a closing in your letter.

Let's Write!

Summary

15 min.

You will need
- paper
- pencils

● Think about your favorite book. Write a summary that tells about the book's plot and main events. Tell about the book using time-order words, such as *first, next,* and *finally.*

▲ Write a summary that tells the plot of your favorite book. Tell the events using time-order words, such as *first, then, next, later,* and *finally.* Proofread your summary and focus on word choice.

■ Summarize the plot of your favorite book. Include details about the plot's rising action, climax, and falling action. Use time-order words and explain the plot as a sequence of events.

Let's Write!

Directions

15 min.

You will need
- paper
- pencils

● Think of a game you like to play. Write directions that tell how to play it. Separate the directions into steps to make them clear. Use words, such as *first, next,* and *then.*

▲ Think of a game you like to play, and write directions that explain how to play it. Use words, such as *first, next, then,* and *finally* that make your directions clear.

■ Write directions that tell how to play a game. Make your directions clear by using words, such as *first, next, then,* and *finally.* Write an introduction to the game.

Let's Write!

Autobiography

15 min.

You will need
- paper
- pencils

● Write a short autobiography that tells about some of the important events in your life. Include facts about your life your readers may not know.

▲ Write an autobiography that tells some of the important events in your life. Include information about yourself others may not know. Use a separate paragraph for each of the events.

■ Write an autobiography that tells about some of the important events in your life. Include interesting details about yourself others may not know. Organize the events into paragraphs.

Let's Write!

Fictional Story

15 min.

You will need
- paper
- pencils
- magazines

● Use the magazines to find a picture. Write a fictional story that tells about the picture. Include a beginning, middle, and end. Describe the setting and the characters.

▲ Use the magazines to find a picture. Write a fictional story that tells about the picture. Include two characters, and give your story a beginning, middle, and end. Describe the setting.

■ Use the magazines to find a picture, and write a fictional story that tells about it. Include at least two characters. Describe the setting. Include a beginning, middle, and end.

Let's Write!

Biography

15 min.

You will need
- paper
- pencils

● Think of someone you know and admire. Write a biography that tells about this person's life. Include interesting facts and details about this person that your readers will want to know.

▲ Write a biography that tells about the life of someone you know and admire. Include facts about this person that will be interesting to your readers. Make sure you use complete sentences.

■ Write a biography about a person you know and admire. Include facts about this person that will interest your readers. Combine short, choppy sentences so your writing is easier to read.

Let's Write!

Play

15 min.

You will need
- paper
- pencils

● Write a play about two characters solving a problem. Give your characters names. Tell the setting of your play. Write dialogue for your characters showing how they solve the problem.

▲ Write a play about two characters who solve a problem. Name the characters and tell the setting of the play. Write dialogue for your characters that shows them solving the problem.

■ Write a play about two characters who solve a problem. Give the characters names and write dialogue that shows how they solve their problem. Tell the time and place of the setting.

Let's Write!

Imaginative Story

15 min.

You will need
• magazines   • paper   • pencils

● Use the magazines to find a picture. Write a short, imaginative story to go with the picture. Use correct capitalization and punctuation. Cut out the picture. Display it with your story.

▲ Use the magazines to find a picture and write an imaginative story to go with the picture. Use correct punctuation and capitalization. Cut out the picture and display it with your story.

■ Use the magazines to find a picture and a write an imaginative story to go with the picture. Use complex sentences in your story. Cut out the picture and display it with your story.

Let's Write!

Formal Letter

15 min.

You will need
- paper
- pencils

● Think about something in nature you would like to know more about. Write a letter to a scientist. Ask a question that you would like to have answered. Use commas in the letter's greeting and closing.

▲ Write a letter to a scientist, and ask a question you would like to have answered. Use commas in the letter's greeting and closing. Write complete sentences, and check for capitalization.

■ Write a letter to a scientist that asks a question. Include commas in the greeting and closing, and use complete sentences. Check that your capitalization is correct.

Let's Write!

Persuasive Text

15 min.

You will need
- paper
- pencils

● Write a short paragraph that persuades other students to read your favorite book. Tell what makes this book so great and why you think other students would enjoy reading it.

▲ Write a short paragraph persuading other students to read your favorite book. Explain what makes this book your favorite and give reasons why you think other students would enjoy reading it.

■ Write two short paragraphs persuading other students to read your favorite book. State what made the book enjoyable to read and give reasons why you think they would enjoy reading it.

Let's Write!

News Article

You will need

- magazines
- paper
- pencils

15 min.

● Write a news article with a headline telling about an event in your school or community. Make sure your article answers the questions *Who? What? Where? When? Why?* and *How?*

▲ Write a news article with a headline that tells about an event in your school or community. Answer the questions *Who? What? Where? When? Why?* and *How?* in your article.

■ Write a news article with a headline telling about an event in your school or community. Answer the questions *Who? What? Where? When? Why?* and *How?* in your article. Proofread your sentences.

Let's Write!

Compare and Contrast

15 min.

You will need
- paper
- pencil

● Choose two animals. Think about how the animals are alike and different. Write one sentence telling about how the animals are alike. Write one sentence telling about how they are different.

▲ Choose two animals and think about how the animals are alike and different. Write two sentences that compare the animals. Write two sentences that contrast the animals.

■ Think about comparisons and contrasts between two animals. Write a paragraph that compares and contrasts the animals. Proofread your paragraph and focus on word choice.